QUEST

a simple
reflection

Amy Churchouse

First published in 2020 by Doing Things Differently

To the extent possible under law, Amy Churchouse has waived all copyright and related or neighbouring rights to Quest. This work is published from: Australia.

Please attribute any reuse of this work to:
Amy Churchouse
www.doingthingsdifferently.com.au

The invitation

This book will walk you through your life adventure, and the adventures of many other people. Adventures that have taken many twists and turns.

You will revisit places you have been, people you have met, and experiences that you have had. Some will have been fabulous, others challenging, some heart breaking, but all of them story making.

Quest invites you to reflect and explore. Please take your time and proceed with curiosity, compassion and without judgement. Discover what might be possible with new awareness and a deeper understanding.

These words have been written to create opportunities. Where they take you will depend on how you engage with them.

This adventure starts with a simple reflection ...

What made you the human you are today?

Where did you start?

Was it a conversation between your parents?
A night of passion? Or a long and challenging
journey of fertility treatment?

Maybe you were planned, maybe you weren't ...
how has that played out in your life?

Or should we go back a little further than that?
How did your parents meet?
At work? While traveling? At a party? At a sports
club? On a bus?

Or was it an arranged marriage?

Did they hang around?
Physically? Socially? Emotionally?

When you were little did your parents take you to parties with them, sleep with you in their bed, or have babysitters come to look after you when they went out?

And what mischief did you get up to when they did?

Did they work long hours, care for other people, or spend their time and money pursuing hobbies?

And did they take you with them?

Did your parents play instruments?
Drink alcohol?
Play sport, make art, listen to music
or smoke cigarettes?

Did they build things, watch documentaries,
go out dancing, or fall asleep in front of the
television every night?

Did your parents scold you?
In what way?

And did it make things better ...?

Make you better?

Did they allow you to do the things you liked to do?

What did you like to do?
Climb trees, play video games, read books, explore fantasy games, dance or sing?

What did you want to learn?

Did your parents help you?
Did someone else?
Or were you left to figure it out for yourself?

Did your parents talk to you?

About what was going on for you?
About what was going on for them?
About their experiences and what had they learned over the years?

About things that matter?
Things that matter to them? Or to you?
Or just about the things they wanted for you?

Maybe they told you clearly how it was, or needed to be.

Maybe you decided to question them and you learned …

Maybe you learned 'the hard way'?

With each one of the answers to each one of these questions, each one of us became more different from each other.

But we are all human ... and we all learn.

Did you go to the local school?
Or a boarding school?
Or not go to school at all?

Did you travel for hours to get there?
On foot or by bus or by car? And who with?

What did you get taught?
And what did you learn?
About religion, history, whales, economics, war,
the Olympics, plants or ants?

Who did you learn from?

Your grandpa? Your neighbour? Siblings?
Some school teachers, but not others?

What did you learn from your friends?

Did these people teach you to listen?
To love?
To question or to fight?

Did they teach you about sex?

About exploring yourself, both inside and out?

Who did you hang out with and why?
How did you look after each other?

What did you get from your relationships?
Someone to hang out with?
Someone to help you feel normal?
Someone to break the rules with?

Did you feel special? Cared for?
Who did you trust?

Who could you trust?

Did you start smoking? Drinking?
How did that happen?

Did you want to or did you do it because it was 'normal'? Or even expected?

Did you fall in love?
With who and why?
What was it that attracted you to them?

Was it what they did for you? Or did to you?
Did they need you?
Or did you need them?

What did you need them for?

What did you spend your time together doing?
Exploring each other?
Exploring new experiences?
Exploring the world?

Maybe you were just trying to get things 'right'.
Trying to make them happy?
Maybe trying not to make them angry.
Were you yearning to be valued?

Did you get married? Or divorced?
Were you allowed… to do either?

If that relationship ended, why did it happen
and how did you feel?
Relieved? Angry? Grateful? Sad?

Or were you numb?

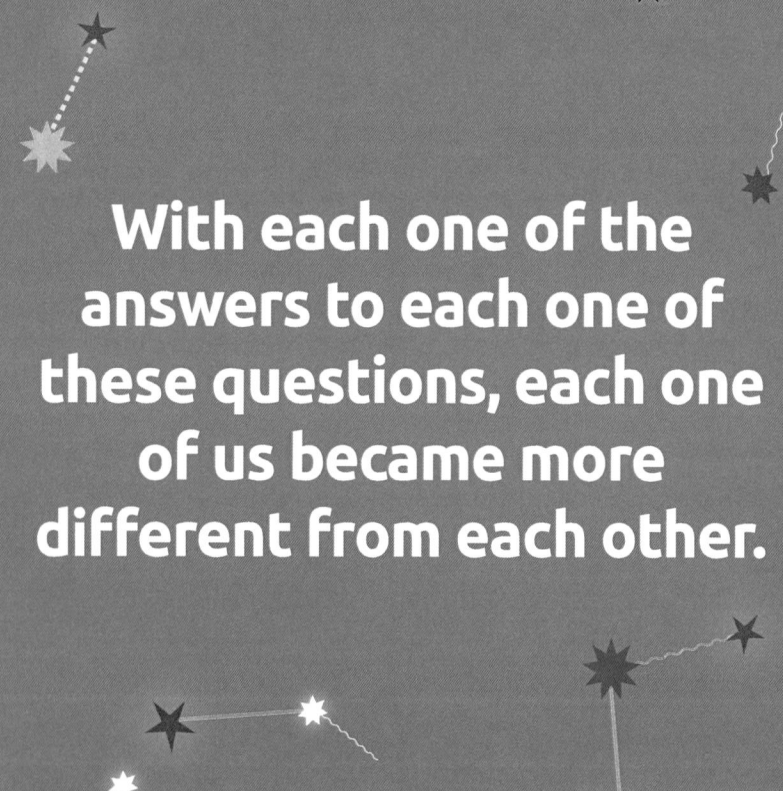

With each one of the answers to each one of these questions, each one of us became more different from each other.

But we are all human ... and we all feel.

Did you decide to study something?
What was it and why did you choose it?
Where did you think it was going to take you?

Did you get there?
Was it how you pictured it if you did?

What doors was it going to open and did it?
What led you to those expectations in the
first place?

Did you look after your elderly parents?
A dying relative? Or someone who lived down the
road and needed help?

Were you in charge of milking the cows on the
farm at 6am every day?

Or getting the other kids to school because your
parents were still over the limit from the night
before?

Did you get a job? Maybe a whole lot of jobs?
Were they offered opportunities, career moves
or the only thing you could get?

Did you get jobs through the evolution of a
volunteer role, your talent or skill, or from
working really hard?

Did you get paid well? Or not very much?
And how did you decide on how much is being
paid well or not very much?

Did you work long hours?
Late nights, early mornings and weekends?
Was it shift work?
Did you have to travel?

Did you don a suit and tie?
Or a carry a hard hat and hammer?

Did your job help you meet your needs?
Or deprive you of them?
Did you know what your needs were?

Did you love your work?

Or did it make you sick?

What did you do with your money?
Were you just getting by, covering rent and food?
Or did you buy clothes, appliances, cars
or make up?
Maybe you bought tools? Or prefered to buy art?

Did you spend your money on expensive hobbies?
Expensive food?
Or expensive partners?

Did you save for a rainy day?
Or for a house, an overseas trip, fertility
treatment or your kids university education?

Did you save for retirement?

How did you decide what retirement is and how
much it costs?

Did you decide to travel?
Where to and why there?

Was it easy or hard?

To leave behind people?
To leave your stuff or to leave your job?

To meet people? To communicate?
To get work or feed yourself?

To understand the cultural norms of a place
that is different?

Did you feel alone?
Free?
Connected?
Safe?

And what made you feel like that?

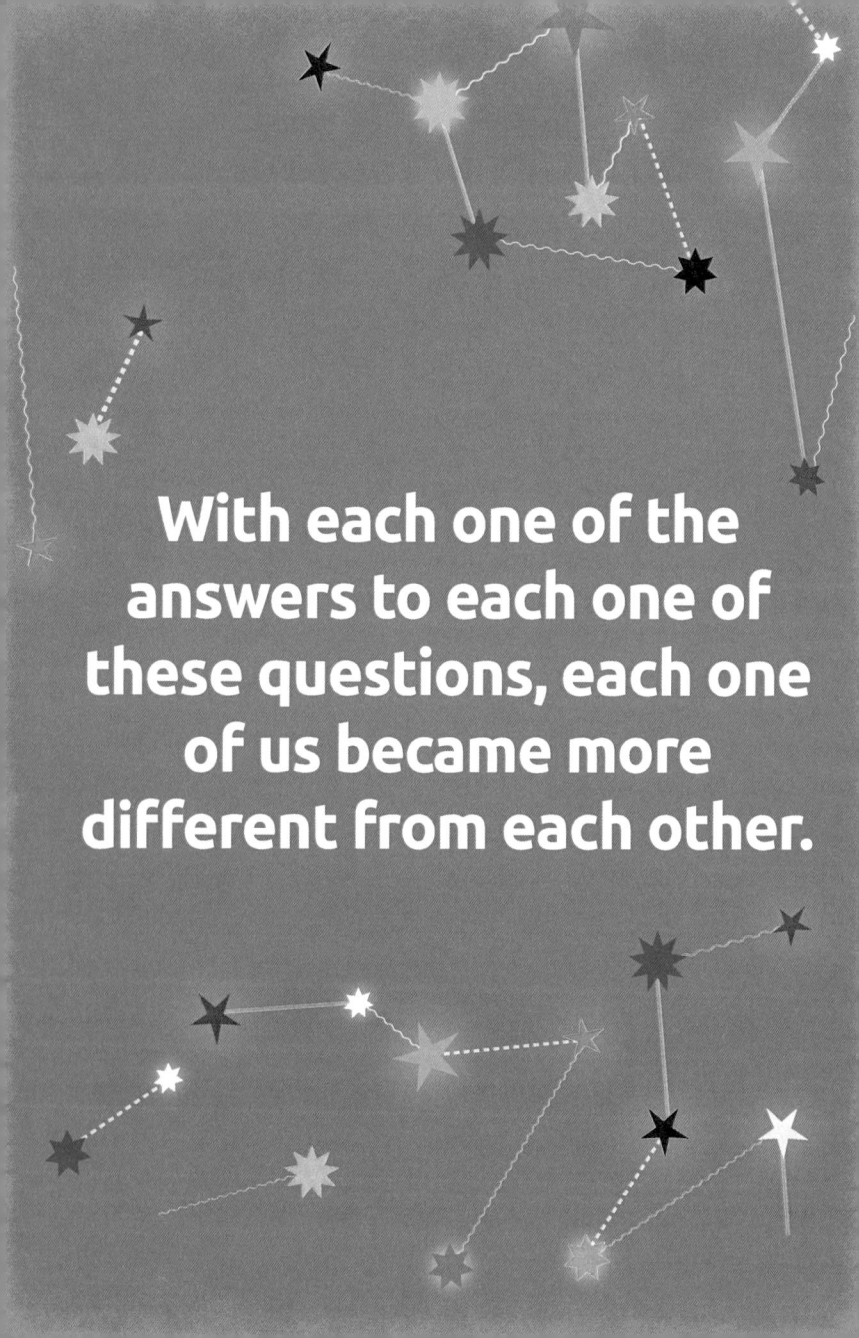

With each one of the answers to each one of these questions, each one of us became more different from each other.

But we are all human ... and we all grow.

How do all of the answers to all of these questions affect the way that we engage with ourselves now?

How do they affect how we engage with our body, our environment or our activities?

How do they affect how we engage with the people in our lives?
Our kids, parents, friends, partners, and strangers?

What about how we think about the future?
Or act in the present?

How do we want the answers to these questions to affect us?

Are we even aware that they do?

Can we stop them or have habits been formed?
Habits that work for us?
Or maybe habits that don't?

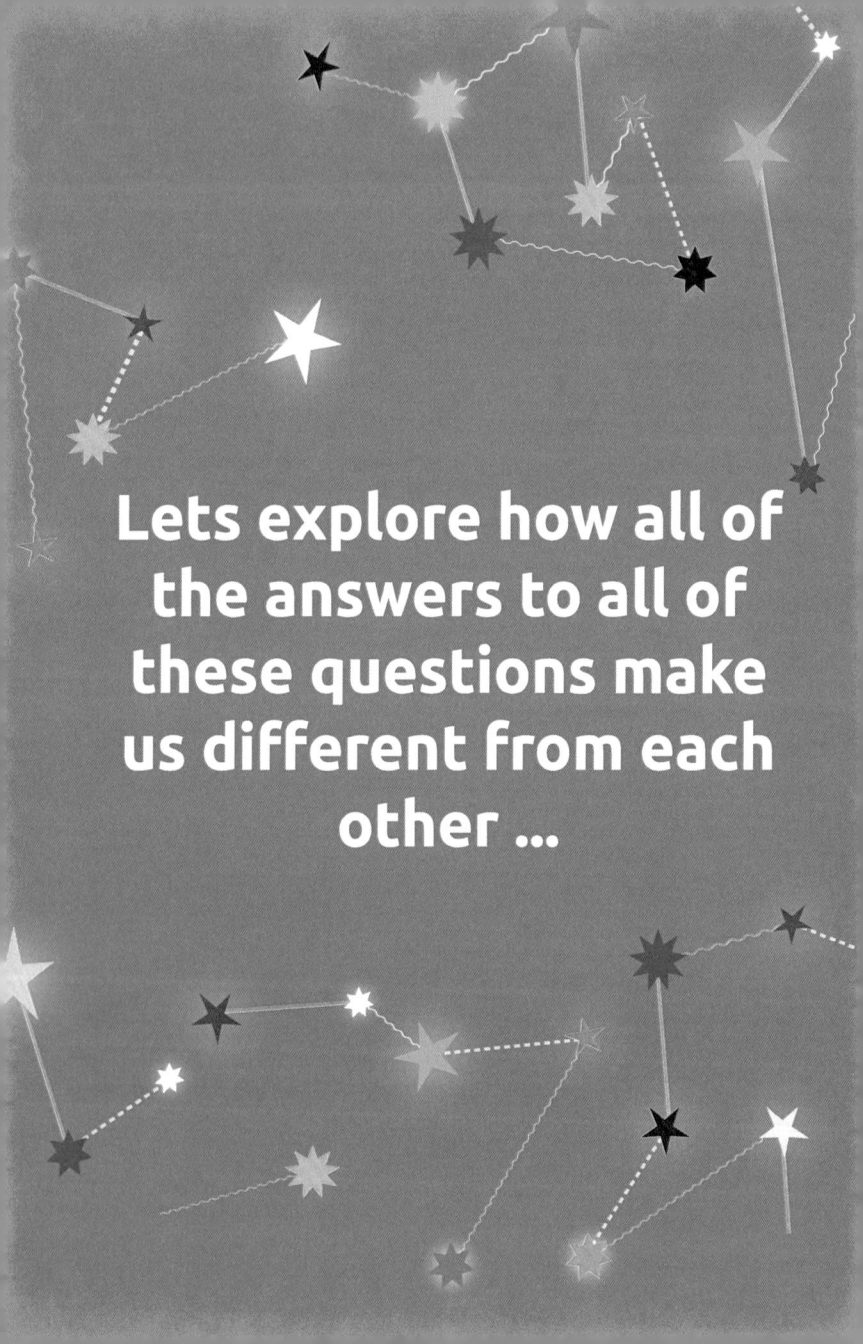

What have we decided to do this year and why?

Because we should? According to who?
Because we have to? Do we really?
Because we want to? Why?

Because others are?
Because it's 'normal'?
Because it looks good?
Looks good to who …?

Because it feels good?
Because it will be a challenge?

Or because it will make life easy …?

What is an easy life?

And why do we want it?

What is the opportunity cost of the decisions we are making?

With every 'yes' we say to one thing, we say 'no' to so many others.

Do the things that we do align with our values?
What are our values?
Have we even thought about them?

What are your needs? Are they being met?
What happens if they aren't?

To you?
To your well-being?
To the people in your life?

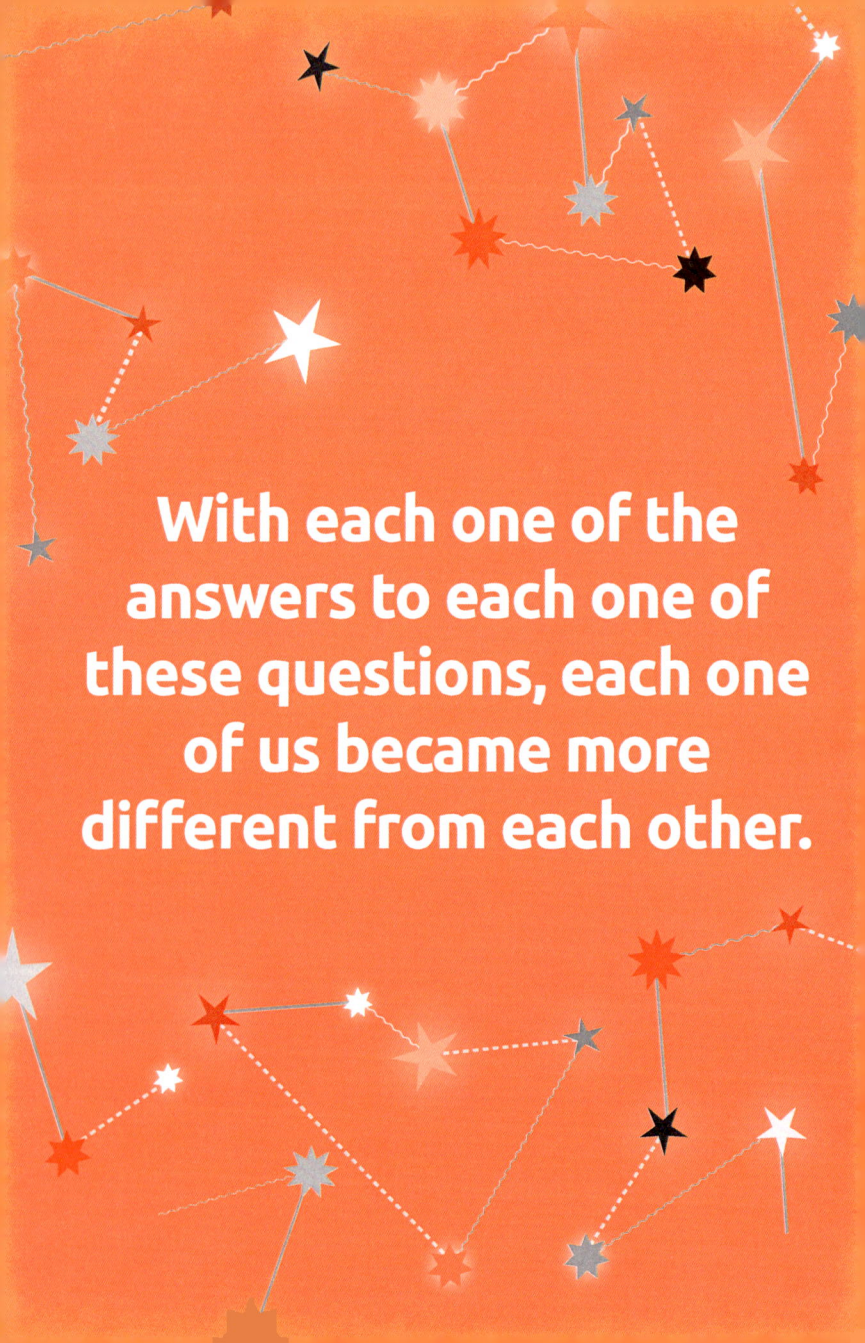

With each one of the answers to each one of these questions, each one of us became more different from each other.

But we are all human ... and we all suffer.

With all of the answers to all of these questions, each of us has developed a different perspective from which to view life.

New eyes with which to consider the possibilities.

A unique perspective.

Formed by all of our decisions.

Informed by all of our experiences.

But also, limited by our lack of knowledge and experience …

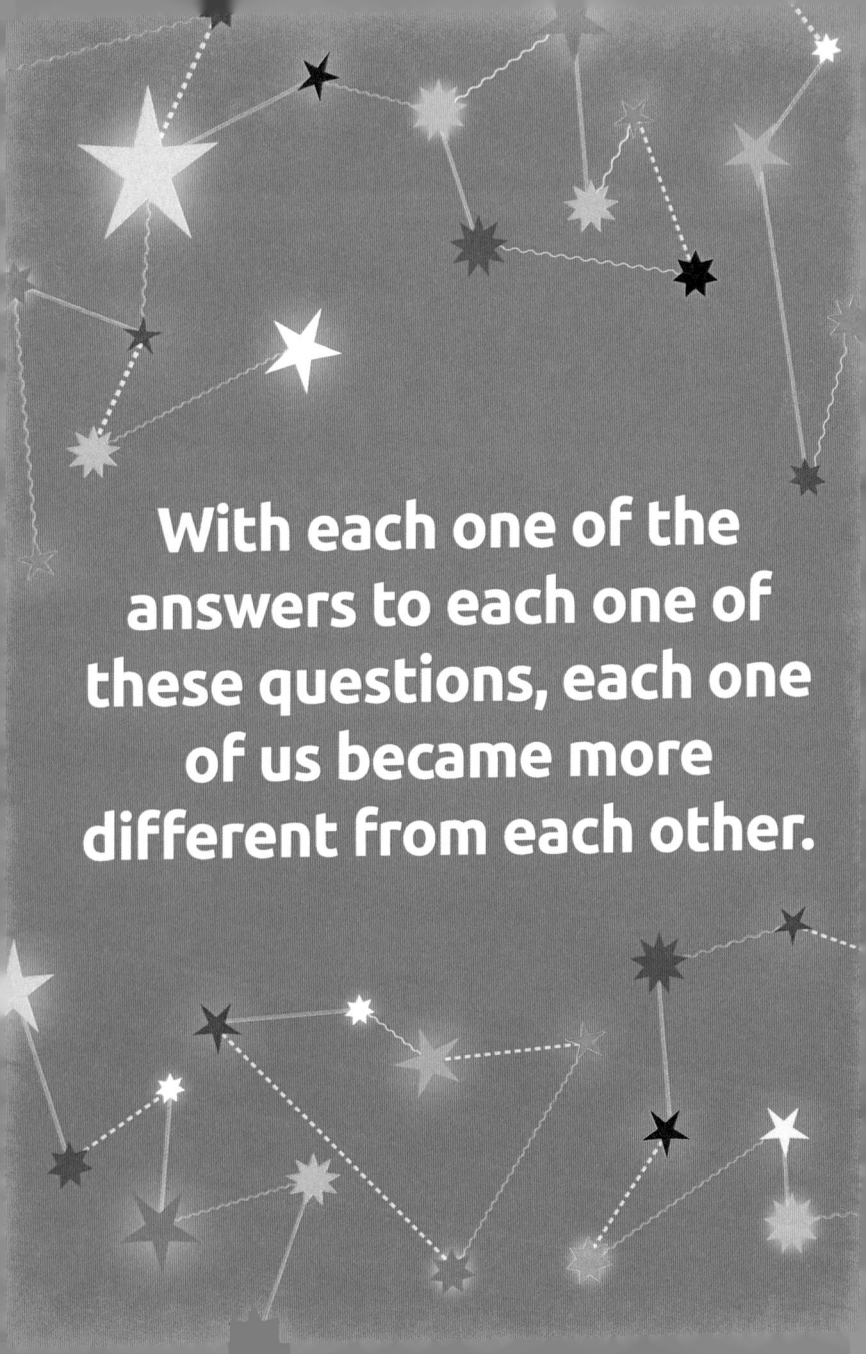

With each one of the answers to each one of these questions, each one of us became more different from each other.

Which makes each one of us uniquely valuable to everyone else.

And everyone else uniquely valuable to us.

And all of us totally incomplete without all of the rest of us.

Epilogue

Where did this quest take you?

Did you dive deep into your life and story or deep into the lives and stories of those around you?

What do you think when you look across the room at someone now?

How did they become the human they are today?

And do their answers to all of these questions change the way that you see them?

The way you feel about them …?

The way you engage with them …?

www.ingramcontent.com/pod-product-compliance
Lightning Source LLC
Chambersburg PA
CBRC090837010526
44107CB00052B/1640